THE DARK ROOM

LETTERS TO KRISTA

RUTH STACEY
PHOTOGRAPHIC
REPLIES BY
KRISTA KAY

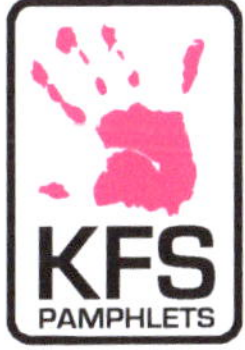

Published in the United Kingdom in 2021
by The Knives Forks And Spoons Press,
51 Pipit Avenue,
Newton-le-Willows,
Merseyside,
WA12 9RG.

ISBN 978-1-912211-78-4

Acknowledgements:

I am grateful to Krista for inspiring this collection and for helping me through a dark period of time. Thanks to Katy Wareham Morris and Jack McGowan for initial poem feedback and loyal friendship; and thank you to my editor, Alec Newman, for all your hard work at KFS.

Thank you to Alissa and Kevin for reading and writing about this collaboration – Krista and I appreciate your words.

Dedicated in memory to:
Logan, Ben, Demri & Layne.

THE DARK ROOM
LETTERS TO KRISTA

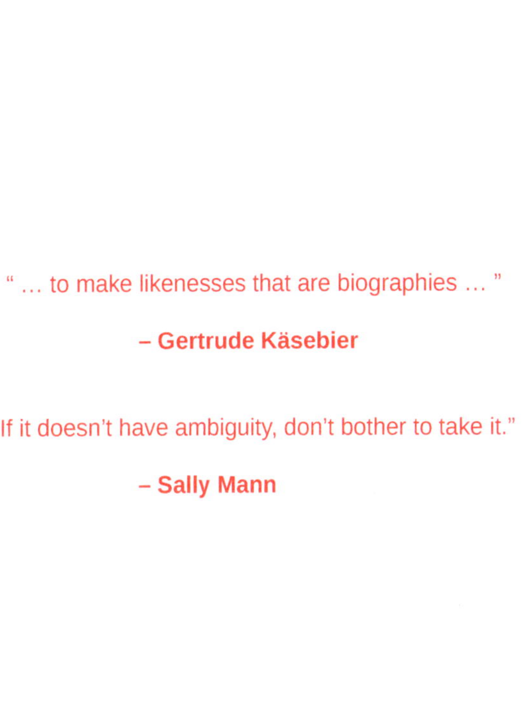

" … to make likenesses that are biographies … "

– Gertrude Käsebier

"If it doesn't have ambiguity, don't bother to take it."

– Sally Mann

Ruth Stacey & Krista Kay

The River Severn

The mind tries to return backwards up the river of life. It is not an easy journey, like a salmon returning to spawn, flapping, and heaving against the rocks. Memories of robust people lie at the beginning of the stream, glistening in their polished newness. The sound of the water rushing down to the sea is little bells tinging in the beginning, how they sing! Then it becomes deeper, more sonorous and terrifying the closer it gets to the estuary and the sea, for we end not at the beginning, but washed with waves into a new place. And in the sea? A thousand sounds – fish singing endless songs to us that we cannot translate and the voices of those we loved are misplaced.

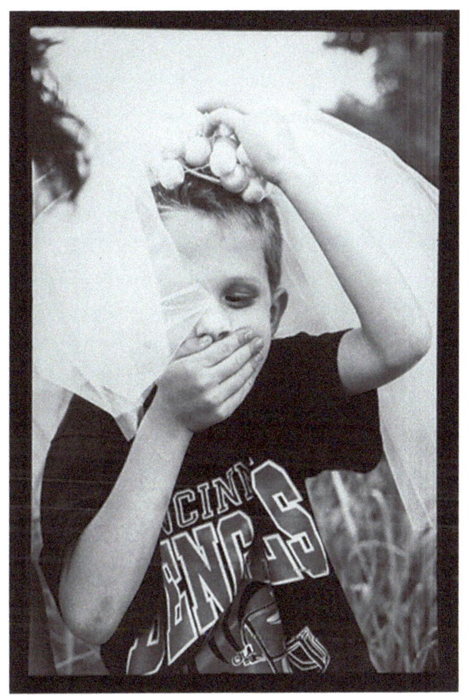

Ruth Stacey & Krista Kay

The Ice Skater

Curious and curiouser. A rabbit runs past, and we follow. Where has the time gone? It leaves a trail of white hairs that lead to images so arresting I remember why life is a charm to be gripped close to the heart. Female American photographer: I have three favourites. Gertrude Käsebier, Sally Mann and you, Krista. An ice skater lifts her leg as she swirls on the ice, the darkness of her hair and dress lead the eye to the tip of her skate and then back to follow each poised arm, so unconsciously your gaze has formed a cross.

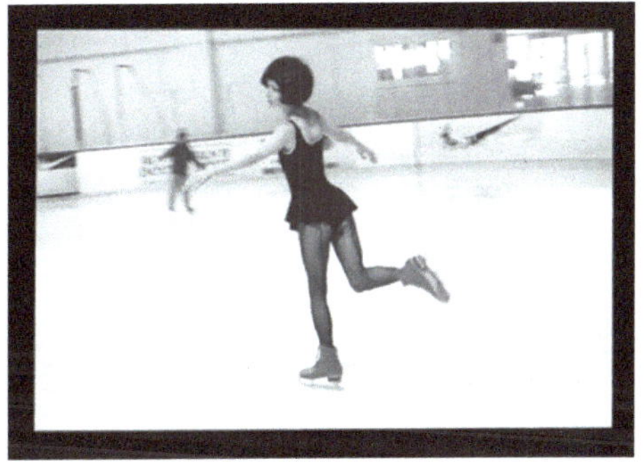

Ruth Stacey & Krista Kay

Hyper Nostalgia

Krista, I have borrowed this title from you. Cardboard holds the souls of those no longer breathing. Old shoe boxes, or something more substantial brought for the purpose, decorated with a William Morris pattern. Lids fit clumsily, after many openings, although that lessened over the years. The chemical smell buried in the layers. Now there is dust, and this unexpected return. Wanting to go back and dwell there. Pen-pal is a comforting word from childhood. Paper letters with stamps waiting in the post-box. We mail our art back and forth to each other. This summer that is what you have been to me, a shoulder to lean on from across an ocean. Exposed, without any negatives.

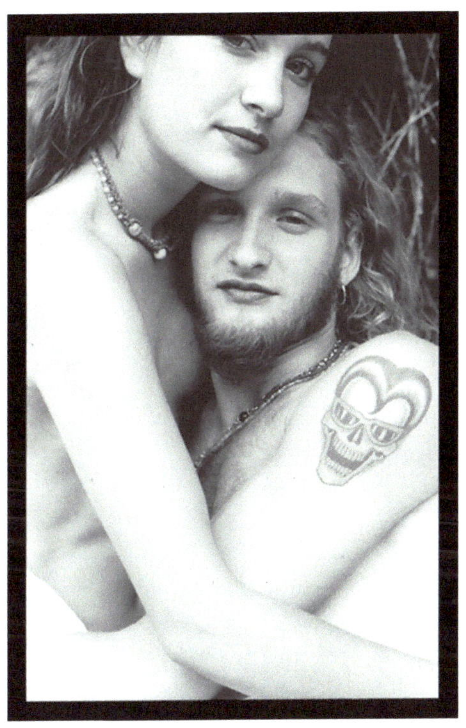

Ruth Stacey & Krista Kay

Palmistry

Palms are being read beneath the safelight. I plunge them into the stop bath to preserve the lines and shadows. There are many chemicals involved with this that you understand, and I do not. There is catharsis in speaking to someone who you have never heard speak. Each message is like a roll of film unspooling. If we could sit together for an hour I think we would fill that time with conversation about artists and making art. I would pour you a cold glass of beer and listen to your vowels settle in the air.

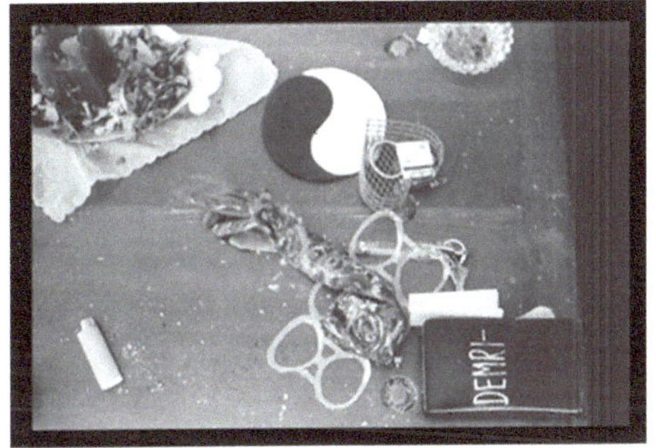
DEMRI-

Ruth Stacey & Krista Kay

The Sketch (and a Spell)

A woman is dressed in loose, creamy folds, with the sleeves calling back to the medieval era. Pre-Raphaelite influence. Perhaps she is thinking about knights on horseback and embroidery stiches in a tapestry. I sometimes long to be living in a time without electrical things that never stop, but how could I describe this photograph to you Krista, without the 21st century magic that will wing it to you in an instant? Look, the photographer is recording the exactness of the moment. The model's waist is highlighted with a beaded belt. She stands with her book and pencil in a field. There is a wall between her and what she is looking at, what she wants. Her considered gaze is still, despite the wind that stirs her hair. The shadows creep forward like paint strokes on a canvas.

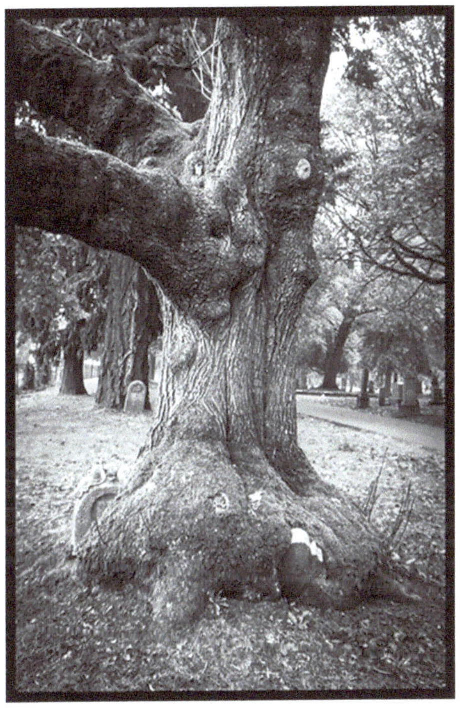

Ruth Stacey & Krista Kay

Emmett's Obituary

Scrapbook of images saved from art college. Pictures that inspired, compelled, mesmerised. First artworks I pinned down that I found on my own. Cut out and pasted in with glue. A boy with a bloody nose, children playing. The same boy in water, his waist ringed with the current, like a river god, defiant face staring into the eyes of his photographer. Mother. Intimacy is such a tender word: inside, interior, hinting at time. Pale orange and tasting of nutmeg. The internet allows invasive tenderness revealing a collection of phrases written in mourning. The words flap – scarves hung in a garden to form a tent. The sepia tones melt like milk stirred into hot, black coffee to become his dark eyes.

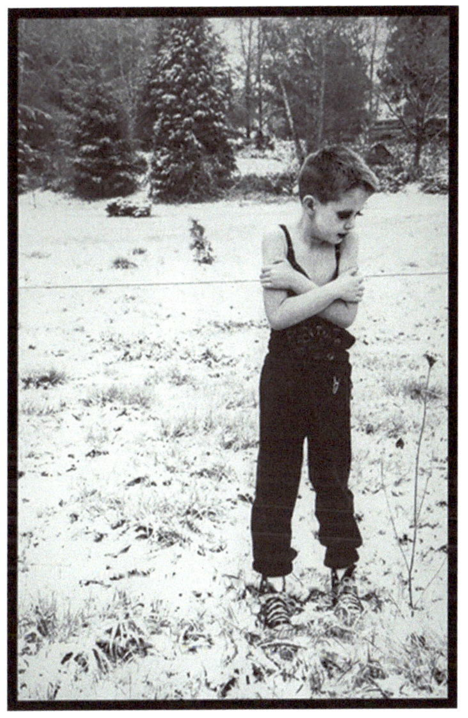

Ruth Stacey & Krista Kay

In-between Room

There are two doors with a space in between. Sometimes there is a revolving door, sometimes there is a curtain. Purgatory is a word that frightens me. I am accompanied by childhood religion everywhere I go – heavy angel feathers glint; that mournful man on the cross; wedding blood-wine from water, and the idea of sin. This is the place you must stay if you hasten your own death. You can never reach heaven. I do not believe it. I am a person trying to find my way down the spiral staircase inside a Norman castle with my long dress dragging on the stones. I only have a candle and there is no clarity. But I do not believe it.

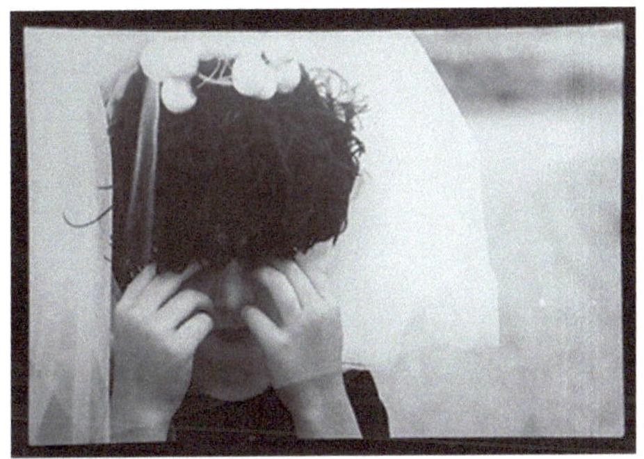

Ruth Stacey & Krista Kay

Submerged

How to leave this place? With Dorothy Parker's Resumé memorised when I was a teen, there is a cynical reaction to each option. The river is damp, but it calls to me at times. Nothing like that chaotic drug death-dance of youth, this is a recognisable illness to be countered. The Severn, with its slow old man river journey winding by my home, only a short walk away. To slip in the murky, dark water and become a siren. Not gold tailed and agile though. A saturated bag of flesh. It is a vile thought that my mind touches like a bruise or a wobbly tooth: the tongue keeps pressing it to feel the pain. Someone would have to deal with the empty fleshliness of me. The soil-rich smell of the water, the blue-orange flash of a kingfisher. The awkward flap of a heron lifting its stalk legs beneath it to escape from our approach. The children laughing as they splash water in the canoe. Breathe, breathe, breathe. How peaceful it is on the river, how lovely to be here.

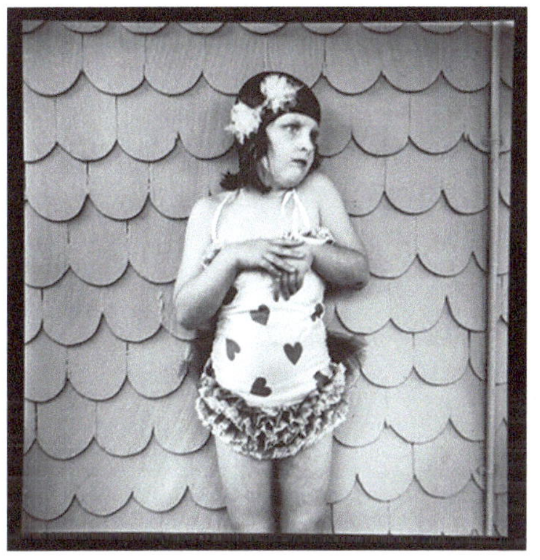

Ruth Stacey & Krista Kay

Fin de Siècle

Reminiscing, missing live bands, listening to our old anecdotes, and doting on lost folks. A different kind of fin de siècle, tinged with punk and flavoured with rave, cynical second Elizabethans, not Victorians. Decadence, make art for art's sake, dance all night with friends, and talk for hours. Was it another beautiful era, a mildewed one?100 years since the last decade buzzed with anticipation and gushed with art; a feverish outpouring. Then the century we were kicking around in geared up to change over again, like a huge beast beginning to rouse itself and slowly heaving up from sleep. The animal vitality pulsed. Not 1890's, 1990's – this was our turn of the century. Shared nostalgia lights it up like a flash bulb.

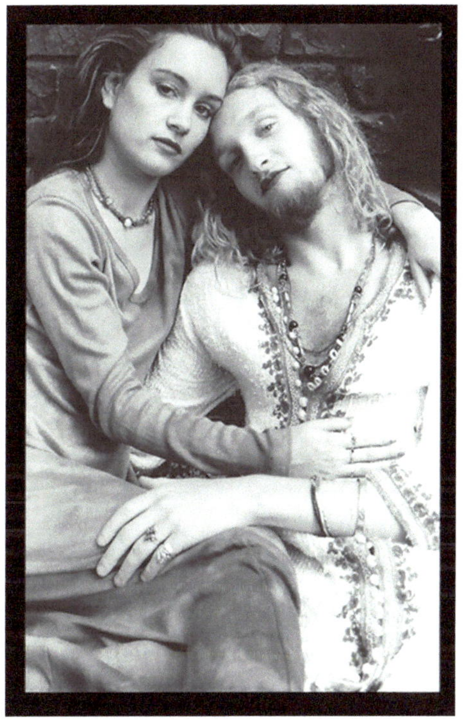

Demri

only a loved one could take these photographs long dark hair is a veil around the oval face, elf-chin, large-eyed sweetness, and the blond haired pensive man dressed in a white embroidered robe is watching her as if he cannot believe he has this sprite held for a moment, the blur of her *only an artist could capture* unfathomable eyes focused on him he beams with an inner radiance as if he were a star *only an artist-friend could take these* tenderest of moments, dressed for a wedding, Demri is wearing a veil, little white pom-poms adorn her brow, *a friend photographs* snowy wings that ruffle a tutu behind her, pan-stick pale face and kohl rimmed eyes.

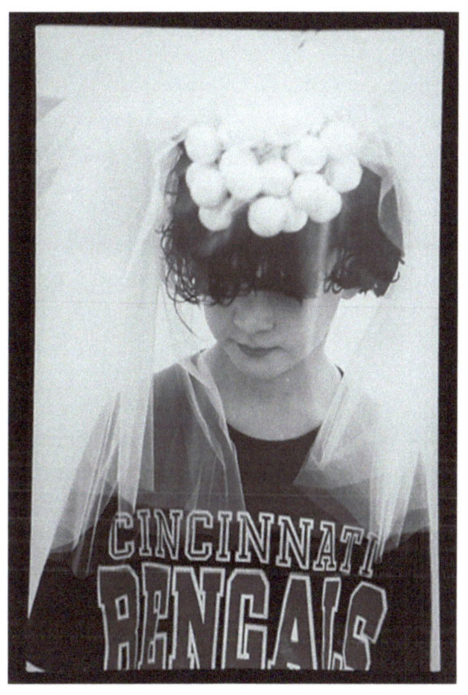
CINCINNATI
BENGALS

Ruth Stacey & Krista Kay

Swimming

My out of focus photographic blurring prints, saved in a box, mean something only to me. Anything that caught the eye. Snapped. Pinned to the film. Unknown until the dark room hours. It floats lazily to the surface like a basking shark. So passive, despite the weight of what it might reveal. Gently swill the bath from side to side to make a wave wash languidly over the paper. Tip of the tongue parts the mouth in concentration, head turned slightly to the left, eyes squinted to focus on darker lines as the image settles into certainties. The body is covered in photographic paper. One day someone will become known to you, like a bath of cool developing fluid, and reveal every mark you experienced.

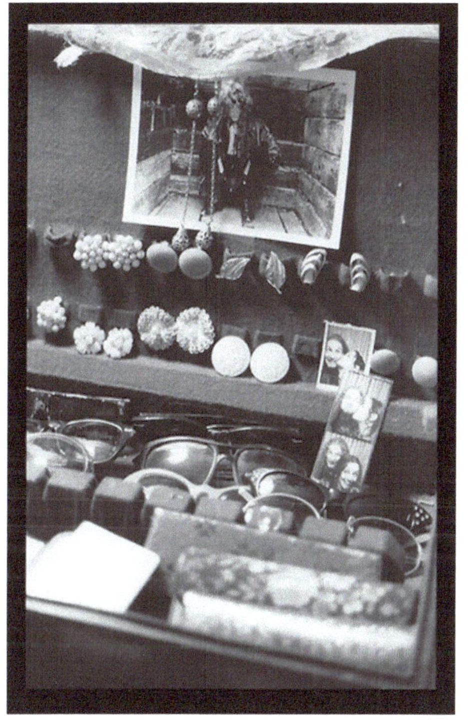

Ruth Stacey & Krista Kay

The Red Bulb

I wish there were a portable darkroom on wheels, hitched up to a dappled grey horse, that I could drag to all the lost places I want to photograph. An orchard filled with daffodils. Climb inside my strange little house and reveal the pictures one after another, lit beneath my rosy sun. Almost glimpse the image I was after. Eat only cheese cut thinly onto home-made dark bread, with spoons of vinegar-sharp beetroot, taken from jars of my grandmother's pickles that no longer exist. Write the absences I cannot find in my photographs. Pat my horse and listen to him crop grass in the night, punctuated by the round full stop sound of yellow apples dropping from the trees.

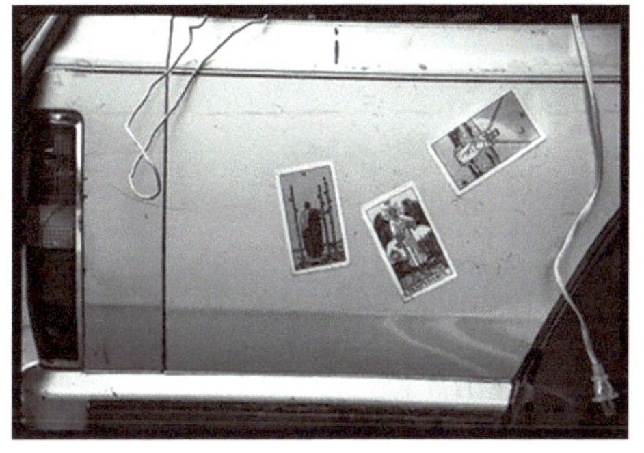

Perchance

oh my god, I love the pink-gold light of evening reflected on the belly of a white bird flying in the cloud wisp besieged sky. oh my god, I love the heavy scent of the maythorn hanging overhead because the hedgerow escaped and grew into a tree. oh my god, I love the soft soil giving way beneath my feet as I walk the path left by the tractor this morning. oh my god, I love the coolness of the air as nearer to the river I get, and the smell of mud rich as rotting leaves, and the desire to cast myself in, oh my god, to reach you now as I am so tired, but I would not be allowed to see you. oh my god, because they say my soul would be mired in purgatory.

Perchance

oh my god, I love the pink-gold light of evening reflected on the belly of a white bird flying in the cloud wisp besieged sky. oh my god, I love the heavy scent of the maythorn hanging overhead because the hedgerow escaped and grew into a tree. oh my god, I love the soft soil giving way beneath my feet as I walk the path left by the tractor this morning. oh my god, I love the coolness of the air as nearer to the river I get, and the smell of mud rich as rotting leaves, and the desire to swim in the cool water on this hot day, oh my god, to use my body's strength to reach the other bank and walk in the meadow there. oh my god, cows, in their lowing beauty, are coming down to drink.

Ruth Stacey & Krista Kay

Perchance

oh my god, I love the pink-gold light of evening reflected on the belly of a white bird flying in the cloud wisp besieged sky. oh my god, I love the heavy scent of the maythorn hanging overhead because the hedgerow escaped and grew into a tree. oh my god, I love the soft soil giving way beneath my feet as I walk the path left by the tractor this morning. oh my god, I love the coolness of the air as nearer to the river I get, and the smell of mud rich as rotting leaves, and my lover who walks beside me, oh my god, enough to make us find a still bower to lie beneath, oh my god, the loveliness of his smile as I blaspheme your name.

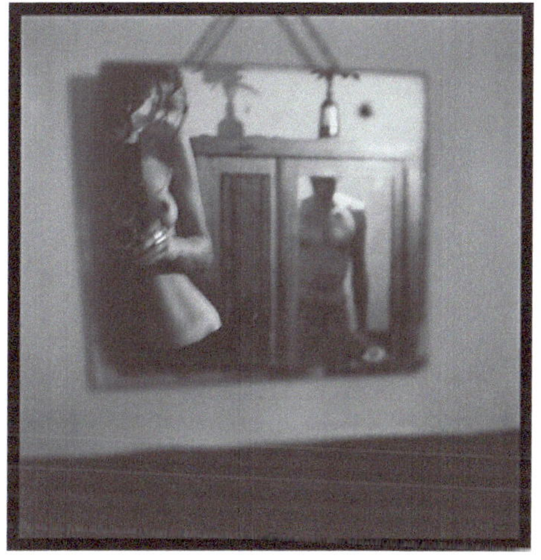

Ruth Stacey & Krista Kay

Joie de Vivre

Rilke wrote something that comforts me about accepting beauty *and* terror, that no feeling is final. And Keats said that a thing of beauty is a joy forever, its loveliness increases. Poets carry these quotes in their pockets like breadcrumbs, to leave a trail for others. A butterfly, a kitten, a hummingbird, so many similes to choose from. A photograph, a painting, a poem. They lived in a heat haze that still blazes now, coming through your portraits like an arrow shot from a burning bow.

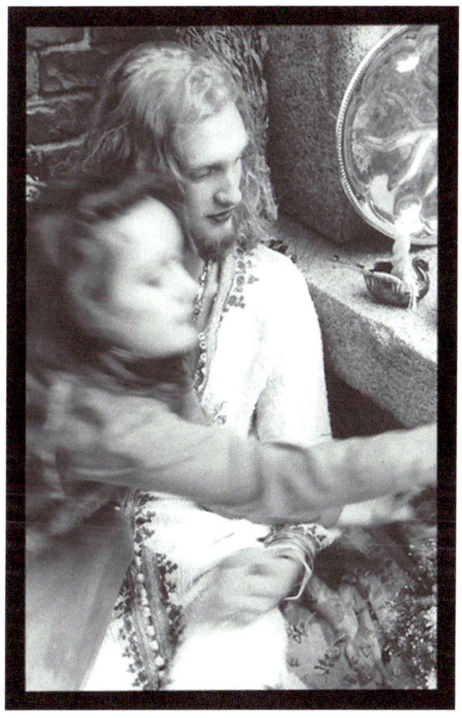

Ruth Stacey & Krista Kay

Burning Melancholia Away

It is cold in the cottage. I wonder, is it cold where you are? Rain saturates everything here so that even the dog doesn't want to go outside. Birch bark is shredded to make kindling. A match is struck. It makes a pretty picture when the flames flare up and do their ancient dance. It is easy to personify fire as it licks and hisses; flame fingers reach up the chimney. In the amber glow half-happiness settles like a tortoiseshell cat stretched out to resemble a discarded scarf. I feel better. Reminiscing has made me dig out an old art folder. The fire lights up the ardent teenage scrawling. A painting of punks, another of dragons. Postcards I made for a project to post to strangers. A hare leaps. There are a couple left and my first thought is I will post you one – we can ignore that rule about strangers.

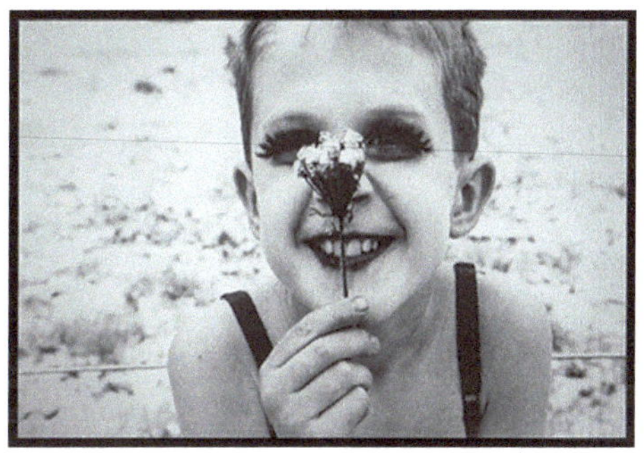

Ruth Stacey & Krista Kay

Anchor

Three stout, grey, badly carved lions sit on the wall that lines the tree covered avenue on the walk to the river. I call them depression, anxiety, and existential dread. Anxiety looks less like a lion and more like a cat, and for that reason, I have made friends with it. The sunset performs its peach-ribboned loveliness. A magical device pings. In Portland you are just getting up, Krista, here I am just winding down. The clocks tick out of time. We send our electrical letters back and forth. It is another kind of beauty, isn't it, the coincidence of us meeting?

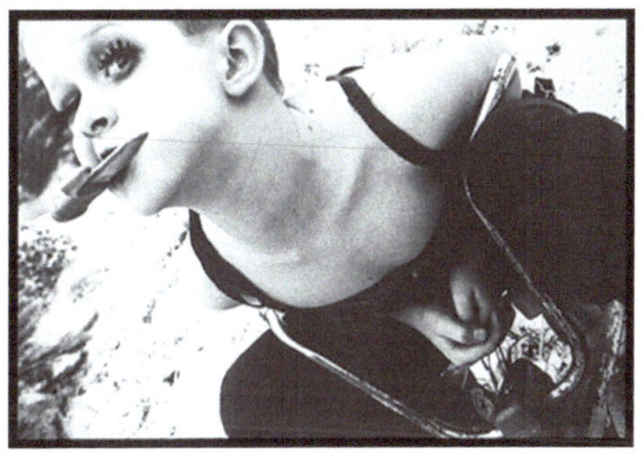

Works Cited:

Epigraph Quote by Gertrude Käsebier documented by Mary Fanton Roberts [Giles Edgerton], in the article "Photography as an Emotional Art: A Study of the Work of Gertrude Käsebier," Craftsman 12 (April 1907), p. 88.

Quote by Sally Mann from an interview on PBS.org September 2001

Paraphrased lines from Book of Hours I, 59 by Rainer Maria Rilke and from Endymion by John Keats.

Photographs Referenced:

Kasebier, Gertrude: The Sketch (Beatrice Baxter Ruyl)1903

Mann, Sally: The Last Time Emmett Modelled Nude, 1987

Kay, Krista : Miranda July at Valley Ice Arena, Portland, OR 2000

Kay, Krista: Various photographs of Demri Parrott and Layne Staley

www.ingramcontent.com/pod-product-compliance
Lightning Source LLC
LaVergne TN
LVHW052310100826
845147LV00006B/723